BE A SCIENTIST
LET'S INVESTIGATE
SOLIDS

JACQUI BAILEY

CRABTREE
PUBLISHING COMPANY
WWW.CRABTREEBOOKS.COM

CRABTREE
PUBLISHING COMPANY
WWW.CRABTREEBOOKS.COM

Author: Jacqui Bailey

Editorial director: Kathy Middleton

Series editor: Julia Bird

Editor: Ellen Rodger

Illustrator: Ed Myer

Packaged by: Collaborate

Proofreader: Petrice Custance

**Production coordinator
and Prepress technician:** Ken Wright

Print coordinator: Katherine Berti

Library and Achives Canada Cataloguing in Publication

Title: Let's investigate solids / Jacqui Bailey.
Other titles: Investigating solids
Names: Bailey, Jacqui, author.
Description: Series statement: Be a scientist |
  Previously published under title: Investigating solids. |
  Includes index.
Identifiers: Canadiana (print) 20200354728 |
  Canadiana (ebook) 20200354752 |
  ISBN 9781427127761 (hardcover) |
  ISBN 9781427127822 (softcover) |
  ISBN 9781427127884 (HTML)
Subjects: LCSH: Solids—Juvenile literature. | LCSH: Solids—
  Experiments—Juvenile literature. | LCSH: Solid state physics—
  Juvenile literature. | LCSH: Solid state physics—Experiments—
  Juvenile literature.
Classification: LCC QC176.3 .B35 2021 | DDC j530.4/1—dc23

Library of Congress Cataloging-in-Publication Data

Names: Bailey, Jacqui, author.
Title: Let's investigate solids / Jacqui Bailey.
Description: New York, NY : Crabtree Publishing Company, 2021. |
  Series: Be a scientist | Includes index.
Identifiers: LCCN 2020045169 (print) | LCCN 2020045170 (ebook) |
  ISBN 9781427127761 (hardcover) |
  ISBN 9781427127822 (paperback) |
  ISBN 9781427127884 (ebook)
Subjects: LCSH: Solids--Juvenile literature.
Classification: LCC QC176.3 .B354 2021 (print) |
  LCC QC176.3 (ebook) | DDC 530.4/1--dc23
LC record available at https://lccn.loc.gov/2020045169
LC ebook record available at https://lccn.loc.gov/2020045170

Crabtree Publishing Company

www.crabtreebooks.com   1–800–387–7650

Published in 2021 by Crabtree Publishing Company

First published in Great Britain in 2019 by Wayland
Copyright © Hodder & Stoughton, 2019

The text in this book was previously published
in the series 'Investigating Science'

Printed in the U.S.A./122020/CG20201014

Every attempt has been made to clear copyright.
Should there be any inadvertent omission please apply
to the publisher for rectification.

Published in Canada
Crabtree Publishing
616 Welland Ave.
St. Catharines, Ontario
L2M 5V6

Published in the United States
Crabtree Publishing
347 Fifth Avenue
Suite 1402–145
New York, NY 10016

BE A SCIENTIST

LET'S INVESTIGATE SOLIDS

CRABTREE
PUBLISHING COMPANY
WWW.CRABTREEBOOKS.COM

CONTENTS

SORTING THINGS OUT

Everything is made of some kind of material. Materials can be **solids**, **liquids**, or **gases**.

THINK about different materials.

- A drinking glass is a solid. It has a specific shape.
- **Water** is a liquid. It flows into the shape of whatever is holding it.
- Air is a mixture of gases. A gas has no shape and you cannot see it.

Can you think of other solids, liquids, and gases?

Solid	Liquid	Gas

YOU WILL NEED
A pencil and a ruler
A piece of paper

WHICH MATERIAL IS WHICH

1 Use the pencil and ruler to divide your paper into three equal columns. Label the columns as shown above.

2 Look at all the things around you. What would you say each one is? Are they solids, liquids, or gases?

3 Look in a book or online to discover which gases make up air. Write the names of three solids, three liquids, and three gases in the three columns.

4 Underneath each list, describe what solids, liquids, and gases are like. For example, some solids are hard.

"BECAUSE...

Solids are things that you can pick up because they always have a shape. They can be hard, such as wood, bouncy, such as rubber, or soft, such as wool. Liquids are runny and have no shape of their own. They flow into the shape of the container they are poured into. Most gases are invisible, although you can smell some of them. They have no shape and spread out to fill the space they are in. For example, you use the gases in air to blow up a balloon. "

WHAT ARE SOLIDS?

Solids are materials that change their shape only when something else forces them to change.

YOU WILL NEED

Some solids (e.g. a piece of cloth, modeling clay, coins, cheese, a ball, a plastic ruler, wooden sticks, paper, margarine, grapes, peas)
Tools to change your solids (e.g. scissors, a plastic knife, a large stone)
A pencil and paper

THINK about how you can change the shape of a solid.
• An apple may be cut into slices.
• A piece of wood can be carved into a toy.
How can you change the shape of solids?

WHAT CAN SOLIDS DO?

1   Test your solids to find out how many ways you can change their shape. Try folding, squashing, stretching, bending, cutting, squeezing, and breaking them.

" BECAUSE...

The shape of some solids is easy to change because the solids are soft or bendy. Other solids are difficult to change because the material they are made from is very hard, so they cannot easily be cut or broken. "

Grape
Pea

Squashing

3 Make a list of your solids and the ways in which each one can be changed.

2 Which solids are difficult to change and which are easy? Why do you think this is?

LIQUIDS AND SOLIDS

Liquids and solids can sometimes behave in similar ways.

THINK about what happens when you move milk from a bottle to a glass.
• The milk can be poured.
• It takes the shape of the container that holds it.
Can a solid behave like a liquid?

YOU WILL NEED
A glass of water
A large bowl
A jar of syrup
A spoon
Little plates containing solids of different sizes (e.g. tomatoes, flour, pebbles, peas)

CAN YOU POUR A SOLID?

1 Pour the glass of water into the bowl. What happens?

2 Clean and dry the bowl. Pour a spoonful of syrup into it. How is it different from the water?

3 Pour each plate of solids into the bowl one at a time. Clean the bowl after each use.

4 How do the solids compare with the water and syrup?

" BECAUSE...

The tomatoes do not pour because each tomato is a single lump of material. The pebbles, peas and flour look as if they are pouring but only because each small piece is falling at the same time as the other pieces around it. None of the pieces change shape when they hit the bowl. When liquids are poured, even thick liquids such as syrup, they spread out to form a level surface within the container. "

CHANGING LIQUIDS

Liquids can turn into solids.

YOU WILL NEED
Small, empty yogurt
containers
A carton of juice
Aluminum foil
Scissors
Popsicle sticks

THINK about how water **freezes** in the winter.

• When it is very cold, the water in puddles and ponds turns to ice.
• When the **temperature** is low enough, drops of water in the sky turn to snow.

What makes a liquid change into a solid?

HOW CAN YOU MAKE A LIQUID INTO A SOLID?

1 Fill the yogurt containers two-thirds full of juice.

2 Cut a square of foil and fold it over the top of each container like a lid.

3 Carefully use the scissors to make a small hole in the center of each foil lid. Gently push a popsicle stick through the hole into the container.

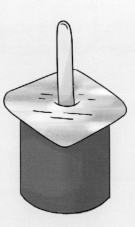

4 Leave your containers in the freezer for a few hours. Make sure they are upright. What does the juice look like when you take the containers out?

" BECAUSE...

The juice turns into a solid because the freezer makes the juice very cold. All liquids will turn into solids if they get cold enough. The point at which a liquid becomes solid is called its **freezing point.** Different liquids have different freezing points. "

MELTING SOLIDS

Solids can turn into liquids.

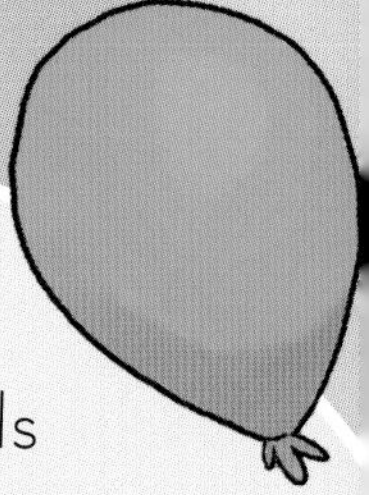

YOU WILL NEED

A pencil and a ruler

A piece of paper

Some solids to test
(e.g. an ice cube,
a square of butter,
a piece of chocolate,
a candle)

4 little plates

THINK about how solids **melt** to become liquids.

- A popsicle melts when it is taken out of a freezer.
- Chocolate melts when you hold it in your hand.

What makes a solid change into a liquid?

1 HOW CAN YOU MAKE A SOLID INTO A LIQUID?

Make a chart like the one shown below.

	Ice	Butter	Chocolate	Candle
10 mins				
20 mins				
30 mins				
40 mins				

" **BECAUSE...**

The ice cube melts quickly because it has a low **melting point**, or the temperature at which a solid turns into a liquid. Butter and chocolate have higher melting points so they take longer to melt. The candle does not melt because it is not hot enough. Ask an adult to light the candle and watch what happens. "

2 Put the ice cube, butter, chocolate, and candle on separate plates.

3 Leave the plates in a warm place, such as a sunny windowsill.

4 Check the plates every 10 minutes for the next 30 to 40 minutes. Every time you check the plates, record on your chart how the solids look.

MIXING SOLIDS

Solids can be mixed together.

THINK about food made from a mixture of solids.
• Oats, nuts, and raisins are mixed together to make muesli.
• Tomatoes, cucumber, and lettuce can be mixed to make salad.
Can mixed solids be separated?

YOU WILL NEED

2 large bowls
A cup each of dried pasta, dried beans, oats, raisins, sugar, and flour
A colander
A flour sieve

HOW CAN YOU SEPARATE SOLIDS?

1 Put all the solids in a bowl and mix them together. How does the mixture look? Can you see the separate pieces?

2 Pour the mixture through the colander into the other bowl. What happens?

3 Remove the colander and whatever is in it and pour the second bowl through the sieve into the empty bowl. What happens?

4 Which solids are left in the colander? Which solids are left in the sieve? Which are left in the final bowl?

" BECAUSE...

When you pour the mixture through the colander some of the solids are left behind. This is because they are too big to pass through the holes. When you pour the remaining mixture through the sieve, only the flour and sugar are small enough to pass through the sieve holes. If you had a very fine sieve you could separate the sugar from the flour, too. "

MIXING SOLIDS AND LIQUIDS

Solids can behave differently when they are added to a liquid.

YOU WILL NEED
A large bowl
A cup of flour
A jug of water
A spoon
A fork

THINK about what happens when solids mix with liquids.
- When soil mixes with water it makes mud.
- If you mix powder paint with water it makes liquid paint.

What other changes can liquids make to solids?

HOW DOES A LIQUID CHANGE A SOLID?

1 Pour the flour into the bowl. Can you build the flour into a shape, such as a cube?

" **BECAUSE...**

When they are dry, powders such as flour are difficult to shape. The tiny pieces in them slip and slide around each other. When the flour is damp, all the little pieces stick together. They can then be pressed into a shape. When more water is added, the shape collapses. The individual pieces separate from each other and float around in whatever shape the liquid takes. **"**

2 Add two or three spoonfuls of water to the flour and stir it in thoroughly with a fork. What happens to the flour? Can you make a shape with it now?

3 Add more water and keep on mixing. Now what happens?

DISSOLVING SOLIDS

Some solids mix so well with liquids that it looks as if the solid has disappeared. When this happens, we say that the solid has **dissolved.**

YOU WILL NEED
A pencil and ruler
A piece of paper
A jug of water
Some empty water glasses
Some test materials (e.g. salt, peas, pasta shapes, soil, powder paint, sugar, instant coffee, sand, flour)
A spoon

THINK about adding sugar to a drink.
• If you stir sugar into a hot drink, the sugar dissolves and seems to disappear. The sugar is **soluble.**
What other solids are soluble?

WHICH SOLIDS DISSOLVE?

1 Use the pencil and ruler to divide your paper into three columns. Label the columns: material, guess, and result.

Material	Guess	Result
Salt	✓	
Peas	✗	

2 Make a list of your test materials in the first column. In the second column, checkmark the test materials that you think will dissolve.

3 Fill each glass about halfway with water. Stir a spoonful of a different test material into each one.

4 What happens to the solid in each glass? In the results column, tick the test materials that did dissolve. How many did you get right?

BECAUSE...

Some of the solids dissolve in the water. They have broken up into such tiny pieces that you can no longer see them.

Some of the other solids spread through the water and make it look cloudy. These solids have not dissolved. They are so light that they float in the liquid for a while. Eventually they settle on the bottom of the glass, leaving the water above them clear. We call these materials **insoluble.**

The larger, heavier solids sink straight to the bottom of the glass. They do not mix with the water at all. These solids are also insoluble.

SEPARATING SOLIDS AND LIQUIDS

Some solids are harder to separate from liquid than others.

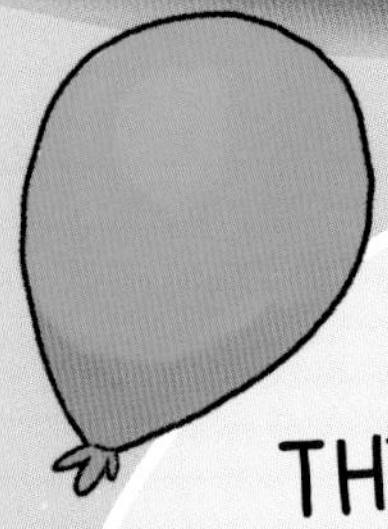

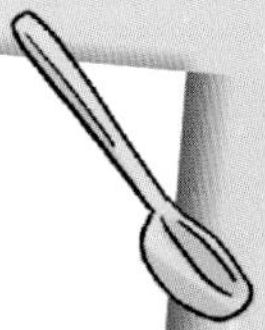

YOU WILL NEED
A tbsp (15 ml) of warm water
A glass or bowl
A tsp (5 ml) of salt

THINK about what happens when you cook pasta.
• When the pasta is ready, it is poured through a colander to drain away the water before you eat it. Pasta is insoluble, so it can be separated by straining.

How are dissolved solids separated from water?

HOW CAN YOU SEPARATE A DISSOLVED SOLID?

1 Pour the warm water into the glass or bowl.

2 Add the salt to the water and stir until the salt dissolves.

3 Leave the glass or bowl somewhere warm or sunny for several hours to a few days. Look at it again. What has happened?

" BECAUSE...

The water in the glass or bowl slowly disappears and only small, solid bits of salt are left. This is because the water has **evaporated**. The heat from the warm room or Sun has turned the water into a gas. The gas then rose into the air. Dissolved solids can be separated from liquids by the process of evaporation. "

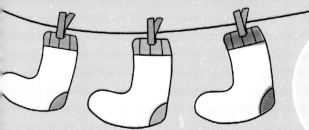

THINK about how laundry dries outside on a sunny day. The sunshine warms the wet laundry and evaporates the water in the material, drying the laundry.

HEATING AND COOLING

Solids melt into liquids when they are heated. They **solidify**, or become solid when they cool down.

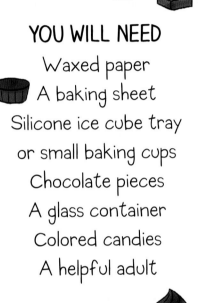

YOU WILL NEED

Waxed paper

A baking sheet

Silicone ice cube tray or small baking cups

Chocolate pieces

A glass container

Colored candies

A helpful adult

THINK about how chocolate shapes are made.

- Chocolate is heated until it becomes liquid.
- When it is liquid, the chocolate can be poured into a mold.
- When it cools, the chocolate will take the shape of the mold.

Can you change the shape of solid chocolate by heating and cooling it?

HOW CAN HEAT CHANGE THE SHAPE OF A SOLID?

1 Cover the baking sheet with waxed paper. Place the ice cube tray or baking cups on the baking sheet.

2 Put the pieces of chocolate in a container and ask an adult to melt the pieces in a microwave or on the stove until the chocolate is runny.

3 Pour the chocolate into the ice cube tray or baking cups.

4 Put the baking sheet in the fridge until the chocolate has nearly set. Then decorate the chocolate shapes with candy and put the baking sheet back in the fridge.

5 When the chocolate has set, gently push the shapes out of the ice cube tray or baking cups. What shape is the chocolate now?

" BECAUSE...

When chocolate is heated, it melts into a liquid. Liquid chocolate can be poured into a mold. When the liquid cools, the chocolate becomes solid again. But the chocolate squares do not go back to their old shape. Instead they take the shape of the mold. "

CHANGED FOREVER

Some materials can melt and solidify over and over again. This is known as a **reversible change.** Others can be changed only once.

YOU WILL NEED

An adult to help you
3/4 cup (150 g) soft butter
3/4 cup (150 g) superfine sugar
A mixing bowl
A wooden spoon
1 tbsp milk
1 tbsp corn syrup
1 tsp baking soda
3/4 cup (150 g) plain flour
1/2 cup (125 g) rolled oats
A greased baking sheet

THINK about how solids and liquids change.

- Butter is solid at room temperature. It melts when it is heated and then cools to a solid again.
- A raw egg is liquid at room temperature. It becomes solid when heated. It does not become liquid again when it cools.

How does heating change some solids forever?

HOW CAN HEAT CHANGE THE SHAPE OF A SOLID?

1. Ask an adult to preheat the oven to 300 °F (150°C). Mix the butter and sugar in the bowl until they are creamy and fluffy. Then stir in the milk, syrup, and baking soda.

BECAUSE...

When the mixture is heated in the oven, all the ingredients melt and mix together so well that they cannot be separated again. The mixture has become a new solid. This is called an **irreversible change**.

4 Ask an adult to put the cookies in the oven. Bake them for 20-25 minutes or until they are golden brown, then let them cool.

3 Roll lumps of dough into small balls and put them on the baking sheet, spaced well apart.

2 Mix in the flour and the oats to make a dough.

27

GLOSSARY

Dissolving
happens when a solid breaks up into such tiny pieces within a liquid that the pieces can no longer be seen.

Evaporation
happens when a liquid heats up and changes into a gas. When puddles dry up in the sunshine, the water has evaporated.

Freezing
happens when a liquid is so cold that it changes to a solid.

Freezing point
is the temperature at which a liquid becomes a solid. Different liquids have different freezing points. The freezing point of water is 32° Fahrenheit (0°C).

Insoluble
solids do not dissolve in liquid. Some liquids are insoluble, too. For example, oil does not dissolve in water.

Irreversible change
is when a material cannot be changed back to its original form.

Liquids
are materials that cannot hold themselves in any particular shape. They flow into the shape of whatever container they are poured into.

Gases
are materials that have no shape. They spread out to fill as much space as they can. Air is made from a mixture of gases.

Melting

happens when a solid heats up and changes into a liquid. For example, when chocolate becomes hot, it melts and becomes liquid chocolate.

Melting point

is the temperature at which a solid changes to become a liquid.

Reversible change

happens when materials such as water and chocolate melt and solidify over and over again.

Solidify

is when a liquid changes into a solid.

Solids

are materials that have a definite shape of their own. Their shape does not change except by some kind of force.

Soluble

materials are able to dissolve in a liquid so it looks like they have disappeared.

Temperature

is a measure of how hot or cold something is. There are different ways to measure temperature. One way is in degrees Fahrenheit (°F) or Celsius (°C).

Water

can be found as a liquid, a solid, and a gas. When water is a liquid, it can flow into and take the shape of any container. If the liquid water reaches a temperature of 32° Fahrenheit (0°C), it will freeze and turn to solid ice. The ice will melt and change back into liquid water when it reaches a temperature of more than 32° Fahrenheit (0°C). This is its melting point. When water becomes extremely hot, it will boil and turn to steam. Steam is a kind of gas. It is very hot, so do not put your hand over boiling water.

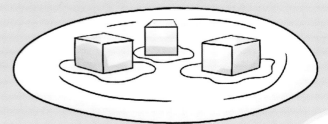

LEARNING MORE

BOOKS
Claybourne, Anna. *Recreate Discoveries about States of Matter*. Crabtree Publishing, 2018.

Field, Jon Eben. *Kitchen Chemistry*. Crabtree Publishing, 2011.

Ives, Rob. *Fun Experiments with Matter*. Hungry Tomato, 2017.

WEBSITES
Go to **www.dkfindout.com/us/science/solids-liquids-and-gases/** to discover more about solids, liquids and gases..

Learn about solids, liquids, and gases at **www.generationgenius.com/videolessons/solids-liquids-and-gases/**

PLACES TO VISIT

The Exploratorium in San Francisco, California, combines science, technology, and the arts in one fascinating museum. You can check out the museum's experiments online on its Explore page. Visit at: www.exploratorium.edu and click on Explore and choose a subject.

NOTE TO PARENTS AND TEACHERS:

Every effort has been made by the publisher to ensure that these websites contain no inappropriate or offensive material. However, because of the nature of the Internet, it is impossible to guarantee that the content of these sites will not be altered. We strongly advise that Internet access is supervised by a responsible adult.

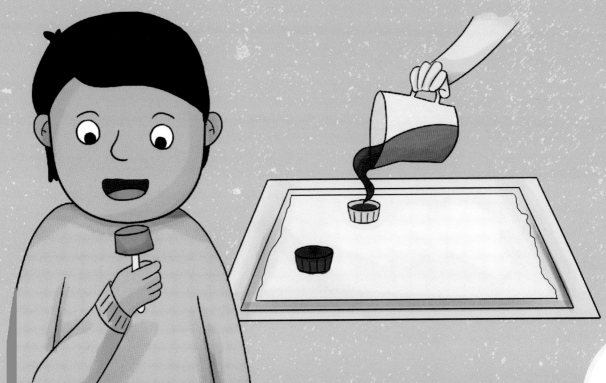

INDEX